The Reflections

Of My Heart

By:

Apostle Vincent J. Gilchrist

THE REFLECTIONS OF MY HEART

By

Apostle Vincent J. Gilchrist

Published By

Eagles Word Christian Publisher LLC
New York

Psalm 34:8 (CEV)

"Discover for yourself that the Lord is kind. Come to Him for protection, and you will be glad!"

Acknowledgements

My heart and soul are indebted to my precious Lord and Savior, Jesus Christ, who has afforded me the privilege of ministering to God's people. I am deeply obliged to so many people because they have helped and influenced me on this journey.

The following are those whom God has sent as ministering angels to my life; some as forerunners, and some as encouragers

My sister Rev. Clara McCalla – As the song says, "somebody prayed for me, had me on their mind, took the time and prayed for me. I'm so glad they prayed for me." Rev. McCalla, I humbly thank you for taking the time to pray for me -your little brother.

My cousin Pear Machen – I want to thank you for taking the time to encourage me when I needed it the most.

My magnificent family – you all mean the world to me. I love, and thank you so much for loving, and caring for me as you do. Thank you

i

for all the support from the beginning of my journey, until now. I am who I am because of it.

My sister in the Lord, and prayer partner , Missionary Gloria Byer – I want to let you know that you are incredibly special to me. Thank you for your help, and the numerous times that we had prayer, and devotion on the phone.

Pastor John D. Wright – Thank you for your encouragement. I appreciate everything that you have done for me.

Mother Alice Goodson - I want you to know that you are special to me, and I appreciate you very much. Thank you for your love, prayers, chastisement, and your words of support.

All these things mean the world to me; you are a blessing, and I thank God every day for you.

A special thanks and gratitude to my Godparents in the Lord, Apostle Levar A. Williams, and Evangelist Jeanett S. Williams – Thank you both for giving me the opportunity to preach on your telephone prayer line. The message that I was blessed to preach was "1-800-JESUS. Call Him up and tell Him what you want—it will be the best call you have ever made for yourself." I came from the scripture Psalm 21:2 (AMP), on Wednesday night, June 7, 2023. Thank you both for your love and inspiration. It is an honor and a privilege to be able to say something about God's precious, and anointed vessels. Pastor Williams, you are a shepherd that gathers, leads, watches, and feeds the flock with sound doctrine that promotes health, safety, growth, comfort, and living a spiritual life.

Thank you for your enthusiasm, insight, and imparting wisdom into my life.

Proverbs 11:25 (The Message)

"The one who blesses others is abundantly blessed; those who help others are helped."

Apostle Alfred Philipps - I want to thank you for the blessed opportunity to preach for you at your church when you were located in Brooklyn, New York. The awakening message that I had the pleasure of preaching was entitled "In God there is peace just for you. Be calm and do not worry about anything." My scriptures were: John 14:27 (CEV), 2 Corinthians 4:8-9 (TLB), and Mark 4:35–39 (AMP). This was on Sunday, February 12,

2017. I thank God for you and that opportunity; you are indeed a blessing.

Apostle Anna B. Thompson - Thank you for continuing to love, reassure, and pray for me. You allowed me to lead the 9:00AM prayer, and for that I am forever grateful. Also, I thank you for the opportunity given to preach on Saturday, May 19, 2107, where my message was "Please be patient and wait on Jesus."

My scripture was Isaiah 40:31. You gave me another opportunity on Saturday, January 23, 2010. My message then was "I came to have church. My scripture was Psalm 145:2–3 (AMP). We had a wonderful time on both occasions. I pray that God continues to bless and keep you. Apostle Thompson, keep doing the work of Him that sent you.

Evangelist Joyce Johnson - Thank you for your prayers, assistance, and encouragement.

Elder Taylor, Jr. – Continue to allow God to use you for His purpose. Keep singing and preaching for Jesus! I thank God for you and the way that He is using you to do His Will.

Pastor Cedric Lauchner – I want to express my appreciation and gratitude to you for granting me the opportunity to lead prayer on your telephone prayer line, on Monday, April 10, 2017, at 8:00PM. May God continue to bless you as you encourage others. Keep doing what you are doing for the Lord.

Deacon John McCall – Thank you for your support, help, and especially your words of encouragement.

Deacon Joseph Belton – Continue singing and directing choirs for Jesus. You are the greatest!

Pastor Maurice C. Lauchner – I want you to know that your singing and preaching has had a lasting effect on me. May God forever bless you in everything that you do.

Sis. Anna T. Evans – Thank God for you. I appreciate all that you do, and for your wonderful friendship.

Elder Eric James – Thank you for your continuous encouragement. You mean the world to me.

Pastor Taki Hopkins – I have been richly blessed by your singing and preaching of God's Word. You are such an inspiration to me. Thank you for your love, prayers, and support. May God bless and keep you forever.

Bishop Katrinyana C. O'Neal – Thank you for helping and praying for me. I also thank you for allowing me to sing and preach at your church. I treasure your love, support, and encouragement of me. I pray that God continues to shower His blessings upon you.

Apostle Press Pullins, Jr. – I thank God for you, and I thank you from the bottom of my heart for everything that you have done for me.

To every Bishop and Pastor – Each of you under whose tutelage or leadership I have had the privilege to sit, and whose ministries have left an indelible impression on my life. All of you have, in one way or another, profoundly impacted my life and I wholeheartedly want to say thank you. Thank you all for your love, guidance, encouragement, support, and above all, your prayers.

INTRODUCTION

This book contains small messages that I have preached over the years, and a few of the stories behind those messages. Herein are some of those sermons that I want to introduce. I pray that you enjoy reading them as much as I enjoyed preaching them.

1 Corinthians 9:16 CEV)

"I don't have any reason to brag about preaching the good news. Preaching is something God told me to do, and if I don't do it, I am doomed."

Jeremiah 1:9 (CEV)

"The Lord reached out his hand, then he touched my mouth and said, "I am giving you the words to say,"

Contents

Acknowledgements i

INTRODUCTION vii

My Way Maker 1

Jesus, You Step in When I Need You Most 2

The Word of God is Your Instruction Manual 3

More of Jesus 5

Thank You Lord 7

God Will See You Through 9

Somebody Prayed for Me 10

You Must Put on the Armor of God 12

I Will Live for Jesus 15

Letting Go 16

I Cannot Live Without Jesus 18

Glory and Praise 19

The Master's Key 20

All I Have 21

Prayer 22

I Am Never Alone 23

Too Busy 24

Enough Time... 25

Thank You Father for the Gift of Life 27

Grace.. 28

The Lord is Good 29

You Must Hold On To Jesus 31

Thank You Heavenly Father 33

Crazy Praise... 35

I Will Trust God Completely 37

Trust in the Lord.. 39

Lift Up Jesus 40

You Have Kept Me, Lord... 41

This Mean and Wicked World 42

Enjoy Life.. 44

Simply, Yes.. 45

God is in the Midst of it All 46

Tomorrow Is Not Promised to You 47

Do Not Panic.. 48

An Invitation.. 49

Uniquely Me.. 51

Stay Focused 56

What Does God Think of Me? 58

A Personal Note from the Author 60

About the Author.. 61

My Way Maker
- Elder Vincent J. Gilchrist

Jesus is truly my way maker –
For He is my bread when I am hungry,
My water when I am thirsty,
My friend when I am friendless.
When I am down to my last dime,
He steps in on time,
Right when I need Him most.

When I was sick, and could not get well,
He healed my body so that you, I could tell.
Yes, Jesus is my way maker.
One day he made a way for me, and I am so glad about that.
I sincerely thank you Father,
For always being my way maker.

Philippians 4:19 (AMP)

"And my God will liberally supply (fill until full) your every need according to His riches in glory in Christ Jesus."

1

Jesus, You Step in When I Need You Most
- Elder Vincent J. Gilchrist

I have had trials and tribulations,
I have had many unexpected situations.
In my life when problems would
burden me down,
And I did not know what to do ,
I am glad that Jesus always stepped in
to see me through,
      - when I needed Him the most.

He is my greatest and only solution,
In the midst of it all.
He is always there to let me know,
That everything will be all right,
Especially in times of trouble.
I am so glad to know that Jesus will step in
      -when I truly need Him the most.

Psalm 145:3 (NKJV)

"Great *is* the Lord, and greatly to be praised…"

2

The Word of God is Your Instruction Manual

- Elder Vincent J. Gilchrist

The Word of God:
Is the only truth that guides you
into what is right.
The Word of God:
Increases your faith, so that you will not
walk by sight.

The Word of God:
Will keep you away from the Lord's wrath.
The Word of God: is a lamp unto your feet,
and a guide on your path.

The Word of God:
Can reconstruct and transform your way of living.
The Word of God:
Is your anchor when it seems like
you are sinking.

The Word of God:
Gives blessed assurance in times of strife.
The Word of God:
Teaches us of our true purpose in life.

The Word of God:
Illuminates your mind to a higher level.
The Word of God:
Is powerful enough to defeat the devil.

The Word of God:
Lifts up Jesus Christ as the King of Glory.
The Word of God:
Brings salvation through the gospel story.

The wonderful Word of God:
Destroys every one of the devil's lies.
The Word of God:
Will even make the simple become wise.

The Word of God:
Is much more than just religious talk.
The Word of God:
Is what you and I need in this Christian walk.
> It is the only instruction manual that we MUST follow,

John 1:2 (CEV)

"From the very beginning, the Word was with God."

More of Jesus
- Apostle Vincent J. Gilchrist

I want more of Jesus,
Yes, I absolutely want more of Jesus.
I must have more of Jesus in my life,
Because He is my everything.

I need Jesus every hour of my life,
He is most precious, and important.
I truly need more of Jesus,
Yes, this is true and dear to me.

I want to be covered, and wrapped up,
Wrapped, and tangled up in you, Jesus.
My deepest desire is to be close to you,
Yes, I want more, and more of Jesus.

Psalm 73:23 (ESV)

"Nevertheless, I am continually with you; you hold my right hand."

5

Psalm 73:28 (AMP)

"But as for me, it is good to draw near to God; I have made the Lord God my refuge *and* placed my trust in Him, that I may tell of all Your works."

John 15:5 (AMP)

"I am the vine; you are the branches. The one who remains in Me and I in him bears much fruit, for [otherwise] apart from Me [that is cut off from vital union with Me] you can do nothing."

6

Thank You Lord
- Vincent J. Gilchrist

I do have a friend who will go with me
to the end.
He is always right by my side,
through the storms of life.
He has never let me down, so there is
no need to worry.
I just keep trusting, believing, and praying,
Knowing that all things will work out alright.

Jesus is that magnificent friend,
whom I will always appreciate.
He has done so much for me,
by His blood He saved me.
I cannot thank Him enough
for His grace and mercy toward me,
I just have to say, Oh Lord, thank you;
thank you for setting me free.

Psalm 136:1 (AMP)

"Give thanks to the Lord for He is good; For His lovingkindness (graciousness, mercy, compassion) endures forever."

Psalm 106:1 (The Message)

"Hallelujah! Thank God! And why? Because He's good, because His love lasts..."

8

God Will See You Through
- Elder Vincent J. Gilchrist

If you are coping with everyday situations and circumstances in your life, you do not know what to do, and you feel that all hope is gone, just know that God will see you through all of it—whatever it is. There is no problem big or small, that He cannot solve for you. All that you must do is put your trust completely in the Lord and believe that He will do it for you.

Psalm 34:19 (AMPC)

"Many evils confront [consistently] righteous, but the Lord delivers him out of them all."

9

Somebody Prayed for Me
-Elder Vincent J. Gilchrist

Whenever I lift my heart in prayer,
I know that somewhere,
someone is praying just for me.
At every time, in every place,
dark of night or brightest day,
There is always someone,
somewhere praying twenty-four hours a day.
All year round, someone is reaching out to God on
my behalf.

I am one with God; I am one with all men.
Brothers, sisters, mothers, fathers, sons, and
daughters everywhere,
Look only to the Father in Heaven, for guidance, love,
strength, protection, peace, and assurance.

I do not need to ever feel alone,
Even when there is no one
available in person, or by telephone.
I can reach out to prayer partners around the world,
any time of day or night.
I find myself always in the company of friends (so
glad that they are praying for me).

The whole world is praying for and with me,
I thank everyone for their prayers.

Psalm 55:17 (NKJV)

"Evening and morning and at noon I will pray, and cry aloud..."

You Must Put on the Armor of God
-Apostle Vincent J. Gilchrist

You must put on the whole armor of God,
Then soldiers we shall be.
Fighting the powers of darkness,
Who thirsts for the souls of the free.
Through lust they try to enslave us,
And silence God's voice in man.
With focus of faith, we shun them,
Avoiding the grasp of their hand.

The devil whispers his disturbing thoughts,
In every language, and every ear.
Tempting all with the sins of hell,
Victims of misery, helplessness, hopelessness, and
fear.

Eagerly trying hard to disrupt God's work,
Evil is showing up in souls
like the shifting sand.
It is good to know that the armor of God
is our divine protection,
Shielding every child, woman, and man.

Put on the whole armor of God.

Ephesians 6:11-18 (AMP)

"**11** Put on the full armor of God [for His precepts are like the splendid armor of a heavily-armed soldier], so that you may be able to [successfully] stand up against all the schemes *and* the strategies *and* the deceits of the devil. **12** For our struggle is not against flesh and blood [contending only with physical opponents], but against the rulers, against the powers, against the world forces of this [present] darkness, against the spiritual *forces* of wickedness in the heavenly (supernatural) *places.* **13** Therefore, put on the complete armor of God, so that you will be able to [successfully] resist *and* stand your ground in the evil day [of danger], and having done everything [that the crisis demands], to stand firm [in your place, fully prepared, immovable, victorious]. **14** So stand firm *and* hold your ground, having tightened the wide band of truth (personal integrity, moral courage) around your waist and having put on the breastplate of righteousness (an upright heart), **15** and having strapped on your feet the gospel of peace in preparation [to face the enemy with firm-footed stability and the readiness produced by the good news].
16 Above all, lift up the [protective] shield of faith with which you can extinguish all the flaming arrows of the evil *one.* **17** And take the helmet of salvation, and the sword of the Spirit, which is the Word of God.

13

18 With all prayer and petition pray [with specific requests] at all times [on every occasion and in every season] in the Spirit, and with this in view, stay alert with all perseverance and petition [interceding in prayer] for all God's people."

I Will Live for Jesus
- Elder Vincent J. Gilchrist

I will live for my Lord and Savior
Jesus Christ,
Because He is my life, love, and my all and all.
I will live only for Jesus who died for me,
My Savior and my God, in thee will I put
all my trust.
I will say what you want me to say
and be what you want me to be.
Dear Lord, I will live the way
you want me to live,
I will live for Jesus, and I want you
to live for Jesus too.

Psalm 31:3 (NRSVA)

"You are indeed my rock and my fortress; for your
name's sake lead me and guide me."

Letting Go
- Elder Vincent J. Gilchrist

Having someone that you can confide in,
Is not only a relief, but also a great help.
A special friend is an invaluable asset in life,
But they may not always be readily available.

But there is one who is always available,
And ready to listen to my ideas
and encourage me.
This is my best friend, who guides me,
With wisdom that surpasses any elsewhere.
This is my special friend, my best friend –
God my Heavenly Father.

God truly knows all my concerns,
Even before I put words to my needs.
Any actions I take, can never be called my own,
Because I am willing to let God be a part of
everything that I do.

God is the core of my very being,
The source of all that blesses me.
I give Him thanks for being my dearest friend.

16

John 15:15 (CSB)

"...I have called you friends, because I have made known to you everything that I have heard from my Father."

I Cannot Live Without Jesus
- Elder Vincent J. Gilchrist

I cannot live without you in my life Jesus,
Without you there is no life.
You are the source of my life,
And the supplier of all my needs.

I need you each, and every day of my life,
You are the lily of the valley.
My bright and morning star and
Rose of Sharon.
It is your grace and mercy that has kept me.

There is absolutely no way that I can live,
Move, pray, preach, or breathe
without you Jesus.
I cannot do anything without you in my life.

Glory and Praise
- Elder Vincent J. Gilchrist

I want Jesus to get the glory and praise
out of my life,
In everything that I do or say,
And in every moment of the day.
Going thru life's struggles
sometimes is hard to bear,
So much so that I cannot understand
how I get by day to day.
That is when the Holy Ghost speaks to me,
Then I carry on and walk by faith.
I only want you, Lord, to get all glory and praise out
of my life,
Because you alone are worthy of it all.
I want you to always get all the glory and praise out
of my life.

Luke 2:14 (NKJV)

"Glory to God in the Highest…"

19

The Master's Key
- Elder Vincent J. Gilchrist

When so many doors are locked,
Or when we are too afraid to knock,
When no one seems to listen,
Or the answers seem long in coming,
We have the key.

We must pray—prayer is the Master's key.
That is the solution, no matter the situation,
The key that will open any door.

Jesus gave us this key, it is ours to use,
As often as we need to.

Matthew 21:22 (KJV)

"And all things, whatsoever ye shall ask in prayer, believing, ye shall receive."

2C

All I Have
- Elder Vincent J. Gilchrist

Lord, all I have is praise because,
You alone are greatly worthy of praise.
You have done many wonderful
things for me,
And you have been incredibly good to me.
For this reason, I will praise you all my days,
I will praise you forever, and ever more.

Isaiah 61:10 (NKJV)

"…my soul shall be joyful in my God…"

21

Prayer
- Elder Vincent J. Gilchrist

Each and every action that I take,
Every thought that I think,
Will be a reflection of love—
still the journey continues.
I do not know what tomorrow will bring,
But I do know, for sure,
that living a life of prayer,
Moment by moment,
is a sacred time with God.

Psalm 25:5 (NKJV)

"Lead me in Your truth and teach me..."

22

I Am Never Alone
- Elder Vincent J. Gilchrist

I thank God for being my ever-present source of
companionship,
I acknowledge my appreciation in praise.
Thank you, God, for always being with me when I
need you the most,
And for assuring me that I am
never, ever, alone.

Psalm 139:7

"Whither shall I go from thy spirit? or whither shall I
flee from thy presence?"

Too Busy
- Elder Vincent J. Gilchrist

Consider a day in the life of Jesus as recorded in Mark 1:21-34. It began with a visit to the synagogue to teach, which He did with authority. Then things got rough. A demon-possessed man started shouting at Jesus. Calmly, but sternly, the Teacher cast out the demon. When Jesus left the synagogue, He and His friends went to Peter's house. But He could not rest; Peter's mother-in-law was sick and needed His healing touch. Later, the entire town gathered outside so He could heal more sick people and cast out more demons. It must have been a tiring day! How did Jesus respond? Did He take the next day off? Did He say I am too tired to go to church? No, the next day He got up before sunrise, found a solitary place, and prayed. He sought the rejuvenating power of His Father's presence. Have you had a tough day? Find a place alone with God and seek His help. Do what Jesus did - PRAY.

"When you feel the tension mounting, and across the busy day only gloomy clouds are drifting, as you start to worry - Pray!"

If you are too busy to pray, you are just too busy!

24

Enough Time
- Elder Vincent J. Gilchrist

Have you ever felt so rushed for time,
That you wondered whether you would ever be able
to finish all that needed to be done?
Whenever you doubt your ability to finish any task,
Let these encouraging words from the Book of
Ecclesiastes be your reassurance:
*"For everything there is a season, and a time for every
matter under Heaven."*

You need only know that there is enough time,
For you to accomplish every goal you set.
We must turn to God first, at the beginning of each
project—at home or at work.
We will feel more relaxed and confident about our
abilities,
When we pause, still our anxieties, and keep our
focus on God.

We can trust God to show us the best methods to
complete any project.
We do have enough time to accomplish goals.

Ecclesiastes 3:1(ESV)

"For everything there is a season, and a time for every matter under Heaven:"

Thank You Father for the Gift of Life
- Elder Vincent J. Gilchrist

Yes, I am a vibrant expression of God's
gift of life.
Expressed as energy, creativity, gratitude, and joyful
living.
And because of Him, I live, move, and
have my being.

This is a gift that has been given to me;
it encompasses me.
I can and will live life fully, embracing it all,
As I participate in celebrating this gift of life every
day!

1 John 1:1 (KJV)

"That which was from the beginning, which we have
heard, which we have seen with our eyes, which we
have looked upon, and our hands have handled, of the
Word of life;"

27

Grace
- Elder Vincent J. Gilchrist

Father, I want to thank you for
loving me unconditionally.
Your love inspires me through all my
ups and downs in life,
Your mercy maintains me in peaceful times.

I know you are loving and caring for me,
Guiding me in every moment.
The abundance of your grace blesses me,
Far beyond anything I could ever imagine.

You love me infinitely, and completely,
I want to do all that I can to honor
your gift of love,
Indeed, you are the giver and sustainer
of my life.

Lamentations 3:22 (ESV)

"The steadfast love of the LORD never ceases; his mercies never come to an end."

28

The Lord is Good
- Elder Vincent J. Gilchrist

Every good gift comes only from you,
My Heavenly Father please make me aware,
Of all these great and wonderful gifts,
And fill me up with deep, deep, adoration.
Thank you, Father!

Psalm 113:2, 3 (RSV)

"Blessed be the name of the Lord from this time forth and for evermore! From the rising of the sun to its setting the name of the Lord is to be praised!"

29

Psalm 28:6, 7 (RSV)

"Blessed be the Lord! for he has heard the voice of my supplications. The Lord is my strength and my shield; in him my heart trusts; so I am helped, and my heart exults, and with my song I give thanks to him."

You Must Hold On To Jesus
- Elder Vincent J. Gilchrist

You may see some people in holiness,
Whom you think are on easy street.
They do not seem to have a care in the world,
And never a temptation they appear to meet.

Please do not let your mind fool you,
No matter how people go about life.
Until God perfects you, it is all for naught,
Just hold on to Jesus and let go of strife.

When you do not know what to do,
And problems always come your way,
My friend, put your trust in Jesus,
Fall on your knees and pray.

Call on your Heavenly Father on high,
Make this resolution—I am going to hold on.
No matter what comes my way, still hold on,
Knowing Jesus will rescue you at dawn.

To win this battle in living life on earth,
And fighting for what we know is right,
It takes perseverance, and patience,
To make it to that marvelous light.

So please do not forget my admonition,
As you pass through this life along,
This is one of your duties, it is not hard,
You simply must continue to hold on!

Isaiah 26:4 (KJV)

"Trust ye in the Lord forever: for in the LORD
JEHOVAH *is* everlasting strength:"

Thank You Heavenly Father
- Elder Vincent J. Gilchrist

Thank you, my Heavenly Father, for
all you have done for me.
Thank you, my Heavenly Father,
for my life, health, and strength.
Thank you, my Heavenly Father,
because you have been good to me.
Thank you, my Heavenly Father,
for always being by my side through life's storms.
If I had ten thousand tongues,
I still could not thank you enough.
Thank you, my Heavenly Father,
for your love, power, and protection every hour.
Through your blood, you saved, sanctified,
baptized, and filled me
with the precious Holy Ghost.
Thank you, my Heavenly Father,
for the blessings of your divine love.
I know that all good things
come only from you above.
I have to say thank you, Father, thank you.
My Heavenly Father, Thank you!

Psalm 118:1 (NIV)

"Give thanks to the Lord for He is good; his love endures forever."

34

Crazy Praise
- Elder Vincent J. Gilchrist

Everybody is always calling me crazy,
Because I love to praise the Lord.
The reason I love to praise the Lord,
Is because one day He saved my soul,
And then He made me whole.

You say I am crazy because I love to praise the Lord,
I absolutely love to sing and shout
to the top of my voice.
I was happy when deliverance came
to my life,
That is why I love to praise
His most holy and righteous name.

When I think of the goodness of Jesus,
And all that He has done for me,
I cannot help but praise Him.
He has been mightily good to me.
Call me crazy if you so choose,
but it will not change my praise.

I know that I have many things
to praise God for,
And so, it is my eternal desire to do so always.
He alone is worthy of that praise.
I must give Him all my praise!

Philippians 4:4 (NKJV)

"Rejoice in the Lord always. Again I will say, rejoice!"

I Will Trust God Completely
- Elder Vincent J. Gilchrist

If everything I thought I knew turned out
to be wrong,
And if everyone I trusted failed me,
If I looked around and saw myself alone
on the path,
I will still trust in my God.

I will always abide under the shadow
of the Almighty,
I will always rest beside still waters,
Yes, I will always rush to the secret place.
I will unquestionably trust in my God.

With all my trust in God,
I know I am always protected,
With my trust in God, I know that I will always be
comforted.
Without a doubt, I know
with my trust in God,
I will never be left alone.

God knows what was, and He knows what is,
God knows what is to be.
I always know what to do
because I trust Him.

37

There is nothing else to do,
and no place else to go,
There is no other choice but to go to God,
I place all my trust and confidence in Him.

Psalm 11:1 (CEV)

"The Lord is my fortress!..."

Trust in the Lord
- Elder Vincent J. Gilchrist

Put your trust in Him only,
You just need to try Him,
You can always depend on Him.
He will never leave you,
Nor will He ever forsake you.
Put your trust in Him only,
Trust in the Lord.

Proverbs 3:5-6 (AMP)

"Trust in *and* rely confidently on the Lord with all your heart And do not rely on your own insight *or* understanding. In all your ways know *and* acknowledge *and* recognize Him, And He will make your paths straight *and* smooth [removing obstacles that block your way]."

39

Lift Up Jesus
- Elder Vincent J. Gilchrist

Lift up Jesus-
Because if He has done something good for you,
You must lift Him up and praise Him.
We waste all of our time lifting up people,
Even when they have done nothing for you.
Now it is time for you to lift up
the name of Jesus.
Take my advice and lift Him up now
and praise Him.

Psalm 9:2 (CEV)

Numbers 6:24 (NASB)

Psalm 117:1-2 (ICB)

Psalm 34:1 (MSG)

Hebrews 13:15 (NLT)

40

You Have Kept Me, Lord
- Elder Vincent J. Gilchrist

I thank you for keeping me,
I realize that it was you and only you Father,
That kept me when I could not keep myself.
You have been good to me,
You kept me from all hurt, harm, and danger.
I know I would not have made it
without you by my side,
For this I am thankful to you Father
for keeping me.

Psalm 55:22 (CEV)

"Our Lord, we belong to you. We tell you what worries us, and you won't let us fall."

41

This Mean and Wicked World
- Elder Vincent J. Gilchrist

When you start living only for Jesus,
And you mean it from your heart,
Know that the world will turn against you,
This, my friends, is incredibly sad.
Even your best friends and family
may forget you,
They also may tell you they do not want to be
bothered with you anymore.

But you have the saints of God
to love, care, and encourage you.
God will continue to work miracles for you.
Allow me to tell you this—the world is so mean with
all of its sinful woes,
That if Jesus did not protect His children,
No one knows what would have happen to us.

Jesus said the world would love its own,
and no one else,
When you start to fight against that,
it will leave you all by yourself.
The world and all its wicked ways
may not like me,

But I am blessed and glad that
Jesus does love me.
He said, "if I be on your side,
I'll be more than the world against you."

Luke 6:27 (CEV)

"This is what I say to all who will listen to me: Love your enemies, and be good to everyone who hates you."

Enjoy Life
- Elder Vincent J. Gilchrist

Enjoy life and do not complain,
Just because God sends some rain –
Still, enjoy life.
There is so much to do,
Each day brings joy, peace, and happiness.
Enjoy life every day that you live,
And live this life to the fullest!

Simply, Yes
- Elder Vincent J. Gilchrist

Yes, to you and only you, Lord.
Yes, to your will and way.
Lord, please continue to give the Yes,
In my heart and my soul.

Whatever you want me to do,
I want my response to always be, Yes.
To you, and only to you, Lord.
My soul says "Yes" to your will,
And "Yes" to your way.

Romans 1:16 (KJV)

"For I am not ashamed of the Gospel of Christ…"

45

God is in the Midst of it All
- Elder Vincent J. Gilchrist

When you feel like you are about to give up,
That is when you should hold on to God's hand.
It does not matter what you are going through,
Believe, and take Him at His word.

The storms may rise, and the winds may blow,
But even if you are going through
the storms of life,
The Lord will always be right there with you.

He is in the midst of everything you go through,
For that reason, why not put your trust in Him
completely?
He is true to His promises.

Proverbs 3:5-6 (KJV)

"Trust in the Lord with all thine heart; and lean not
unto thine own understanding. In all thy ways
acknowledge him, and He will direct thy paths."

46

Tomorrow Is Not Promised to You
- Elder Vincent J. Gilchrist

People think that they have plenty of time,
Not realizing that they should not put off until
tomorrow what can be done today.
The time to get right is now,
Life is too short; you must give Jesus
your life now.
Whoever it may be, do it while you still have breath,
and blood in your veins.

I do not know who this is for,
But I do know that God knows everything,
About you, and about everyone,
Take my advice my friends, and give
your life to Jesus.
You will not regret it, because tomorrow is not
promised to any of us.

Do Not Panic
- Elder Vincent J. Gilchrist

When you have done all that you can do,
Do not try to do anything else—just stand.
Relax, sit still, be quiet, and do not
fuss or panic.
Because you have done everything possible,
Now leave the rest to God.
He will always be there with you, through any
trouble that comes your way.
Simply, do not panic.

Psalm 34:19 (AMP)

"Many hardships *and* perplexing circumstances
confront the righteous, But the Lord rescues him from
them all."

48

An Invitation
- Elder Vincent J. Gilchrist

Since Spring is here, we would like to encourage you to enjoy the pleasures of gardening...but with a twist. We invite you to grow a special, one-of-a-kind garden—your own spiritual garden. This is not an earthly garden that grows for a brief time, blossoms, and then disappears. Rather, it is a garden of higher consciousness, which continues to grow as long as we tend to it.

In many ways, growing your spiritual garden is much like growing an earthly garden. Both include planting, cultivating, nourishing, weeding, and waiting in faith. Although the entire process of growing any kind of garden can be enjoyable in itself, the best part is usually at the end, isn't it? That is when we enjoy the fruits of our labor.

An earthly garden presents a harvest of colorful flowers or nutritious vegetables, or fruits. The harvest of a spiritual garden is *"the fruit of the spirit: love, joy, peace, patience, kindness, generosity, faithfulness, gentleness, and self-control."* (Galatians 5:22-23, NKJV).

49

As you grow your own spiritual garden, my dear friends, your spirit will be renewed; your life will be empowered. And you will bloom, fully where God has planted you.

Uniquely Me
- Apostle Vincent J. Gilchrist

God's perfect plan for this world includes me. I remind myself of this, and celebrate in Him, because I am indeed important, and worthy—I am somebody. I know that I have something to offer this world, I look for it, find it, and then use it. I am amazingly special—I see it, know it, and work to show it.

I am made in the image/likeness of God, and contained within that image/likeness are seeds of greatness and potential perfection. I am uniquely me—confident of my divine gifts. I accept and give thanks to God, for that uniqueness. I recognize my special abilities, and let my light shine brightly.

God is perfect life, perfect wisdom. and perfect love. I guide myself in the direction of that perfection, as I look for and find those God-like qualities within myself.
I am health and wholeness personified; energetic, and vital. I am intelligent and wise in all my ways, and cooperative, kind, and compassionate in all my relations.

51

I am moving in the direction of perfection, and stirring to reach that higher mark. I have work to do, and I do it. When I consider my whole being, I discover that I am physically, spiritually, and mentally, masterfully made by the great designer—the Almighty God. He has molded me amazingly unique.

I am a special gift from the Creator. My brain is a powerhouse of energy that communicates signals to all parts of my body, skillfully orchestrating every movement that I make. I am mentally alert and capable of receiving and achieving inspired ideas.

I dedicate all of my thoughts to the full awareness of God's presence. I am so glad to know that God is forever available to me, as I make myself available to Him. I attentively listen and watch for His direction. In all the world there is nobody that is just like me.

From the beginning, there has never been another like me. No one has my smile, eyes, nose, hair, hands, or my voice. I am both special and amazing. No other has my handwriting, taste in food, music, or art. No one sees things exactly as I do, nor laughs, or cries like me.

What provokes laughter or tears in me, would not cause an identical reaction in someone else.

My situational reactions would not be the same either. I am the only one in all of creation with my set of abilities. There will be some that may be better particular things, but they would not encompass my combination of talents, ideas, abilities, and emotions.

Like a room full of musical instruments, some can be played alone, but the sound is much better when played together—as in an orchestra. In all of eternity, there is not another like me. I am as rare as the Lord made me; and in all that rarity is great value. I need not imitate others, but I will celebrate and accept my differentness.

It was not an accident that I was made this way. God created me this way for a special purpose. He has a job for me that no one else can perform like I would. Out of the billions of applicants, I am the only one qualified with the right combination of qualities. I am something and someone special, and I am glad that God made me. My desire is to continue to be special and amazing!

Psalm 139:14-17 (MSG)

"I thank you, High God—you're breathtaking! Body and soul, I am marvelously made! I worship in adoration—what a creation! You know me inside and out, you know every bone in my body; You know exactly how I was made, bit by bit, how I was sculpted from nothing into something. Like an open book, you watched me grow from conception to birth; all the stages of my life were spread out before you, The days of my life all prepared before I'd even lived one day. 17 Your thoughts—how rare, how beautiful! God, I'll never comprehend them!

54

Ephesians 2:10 (ICB)

"God has made us what we are. In Christ Jesus, God made us new people so that we would do good works. God had planned in advance those good works for us. He had planned for us to live our lives doing them."

Stay Focused
- Elder Vincent J. Gilchrist

Stay focused on Jesus; always keep your mind focused only on Him every minute of the day, and every second of every hour of your life. Why? Because if you do not stay focused on Him, your mind will focus on other things that it should not.

Do not focus on problems, situations, or circumstances. Instead, keep your mind and heart focused only on Jesus. He will make everything all right.

Take my advice and stay focused!

Hebrews 12:2 (NKJV)

"looking unto Jesus the author and finisher of *our* faith..."

56

1 Chronicle 29:13 (AMP)

"Now therefore, our God, we thank You, and praise Your glorious name."

What Does God Think of Me?
- Elder Vincent J. Gilchrist

The answer to the question "what does God think of me?" depends on your answer to another to another question – what do YOU think of Jesus Christ?

If you believe that Jesus is the Son of God, who took the punishment that you deserve for sins, and if you have personally expressed your trust in Him as your only hope of salvation, then you are a citizen of Heaven, and also a part of God's family.

God sees you as His child; you must live up to your new name and position. How have you been doing with that? Are you living as a citizen of Heaven, growing in your Christian walk, becoming more like Christ?

If you are not, then there is work that you must do. You must confess your failures to God, and then depend on the Holy Spirit to help you grow in obedience.

But what if you have never trusted Christ as your Savior? Then God thinks of you as alienated from Him (Col. 1:21), spiritually dead (Eph, 2:1), destined for judgement (John 3:18); (Rev. 20:11-15).

Yet, He loves you and wants to rescue you from the eternal consequences of sin (John 3:16-17).

My friend, if this describes you, what should you do? Acknowledge that you are a sinner, and have the inability to save yourself. You must call on Jesus Christ! Place your trust in Him alone as the Savior who died for you. Ask Him for the gift of forgiveness of your sin (Eph. 2:8-10).

The Bible says:

"As many as received Him, to them He gave the right to become children of God, to those who believe in His name." **(John 1:12).**

A Personal Note from the Author

Dear Reader,

These poems have been a great blessing to me, and I hope that they are uplifting to you. Writing them has been such an inspiration to me, and I sincerely pray that you have found encouragement, and blessings as you turned the pages.

Yours truly,

Apostle Vincent J. Gilchrist

About the Author

Apostle Vincent J. Gilchrist is a native of Brooklyn N.Y. He is a kind, loving, and anointed gospel soloist, author, and preacher, who loves to spread the Word of God. His desire is to ensure that men, women, and children come to know Jesus as their Savior.

From childhood, writing has always been something that he loves to do. He is passionate to share Jesus with the world, and open up a dialogue of faith through his writing.

Other Books by the Author

I Must Preach This Magnificent Gospel
Inspirational Thoughts to Comfort Your Heart
Sermons in Poetic Form
The Stories and Lessons Behind the Sermons
Letters to My Mother

Available online at
https://eaglespublisher.com

www.ingramcontent.com/pod-product-compliance
Lightning Source LLC
Chambersburg PA
CBHW060419050426
42449CB00009B/2028